piano / vocal / guitar

T3-BRJ-573

Butterfly Kisses
& Other Contemporary
Christian Favorites

ISBN 0-7935-8601-1

HAL•LEONARD®
CORPORATION
7777 W. BLUEMOUND RD. P.O. BOX 13819 MILWAUKEE, WI 53213

Visit Hal Leonard Online at
www.halleonard.com

ADDICTIVE LOVE

Words and Music by KEITH THOMAS,
BEBE WINANS and CECE WINANS

CHILDREN OF THE WORLD

Words and Music by AMY GRANT,
WAYNE KIRKPATRICK and TOMMY SIMS

*Vocal written one octave higher than sung.

To Coda ⊕

BUTTERFLY KISSES

Words and Music by RANDY THOMAS
and BOB CARLISLE

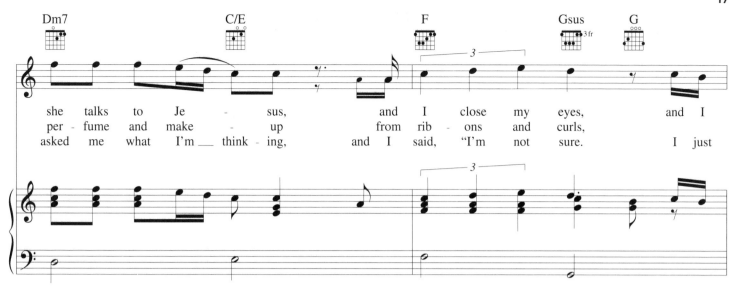

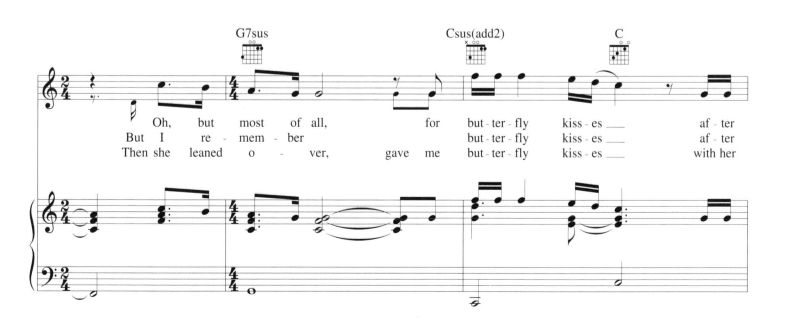

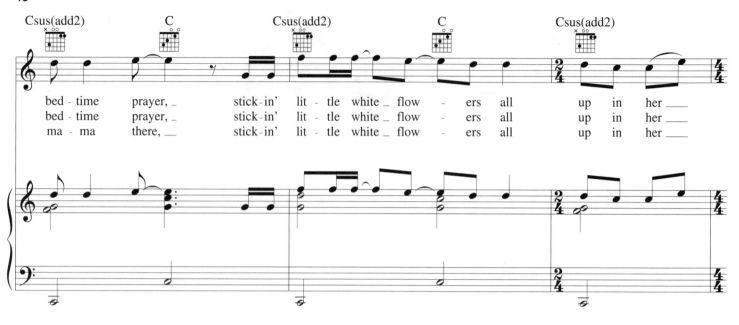

bed - time prayer, _ stick-in' lit - tle white _ flow - ers all up in her ___
bed - time prayer, _ stick-in' lit - tle white _ flow - ers all up in her ___
ma - ma there, _ stick-in' lit - tle white _ flow - ers all up in her ___

hair.   "Walk be - side ___ the po - ny, dad - dy, it's
hair.   "You know how much ___ I love ___ you, dad - dy, but if
hair.   "Walk me down ___ the aisle, ___ dad - dy, it's

my first ride. ___   I know the cake _ looks fun - ny, dad - dy, but
you don't mind, _   I'm on - ly goin' _ to kiss ___ you on ___ the
just a - bout time. Does my wed - ding gown _ look pret - ty, dad - dy? Dad -

CRUCIFIED WITH CHRIST

Words and Music by DAVE CLARK, DON KOCH,
DENISE PHILLIPS and RANDY PHILLIPS

HEAVEN

Words and Music by KEITH THOMAS
and BEBE WINANS

Male 1. Now____ that it's o - ver   there's no more
Female 2. There____ are in - struc - tions   that__ we must

be no more cry - ing.___ Yeah___ 'cause He___ is the light,

count - ing the days when we meet in___ that place.___

Will - ing to die___ for.___ Oo___

(1st time only)

(vocal ad lib.)

Repeat and fade

FREEDOM

Words and Music by LOWELL ALEXANDER
and GEOFFREY THURMAN

GOD IS IN CONTROL

Words and Music by
TWILA PARIS

Steady, with drive

This is __ no time for
His - to - ry march - es

fear. This is __ a time for __ faith and de - ter - min - a - tion.
on. There is __ a bot - tom line drawn a - cross the __ a - ges.

God is in __ con-trol. __ Oh, _____ God is in __ con-trol.

HEAVEN IN THE REAL WORLD

Words and Music by
STEVEN CURTIS CHAPMAN

I saw it a - gain __
To stand in the pour -

I LOVE THE LORD

Words and Music by
RICHARD SMALLWOOD

Very slowly

throne.   I'll has - ten to His ___ throne.

HELPING HAND

Words and Music by TOMMY SIMS,
AMY GRANT and BEVERLY DARNALL

HONOR AND PRAISE

Words and Music by
TWILA PARIS

Right - **eous** and ho - ly, in all of Your
Fill - ing the tem - ple, the work of Your

ways; }
grace; }

we come be - fore You with hon - or and

IN THE LIGHT

Words and Music by
CHARLIE PEACOCK

Briskly

I keep try-in' to find ___ a life ___ on my
ease of self ___ runs through ___ my blood; ___ it's a

own, a-part from You. ___ I am the king of ex-
can-cer fa-tal to ___ my soul. ___ Ev-'ry at-tempt on my be-

cus - es; ___ I've got one for ev- 'ry self-ish thing I do.
half has ___ failed ___ to bring this sick-ness un-der con-trol. ___ Tell me,

JESUS WILL STILL BE THERE

Words and Music by JOHN MANDEVILLE
and ROBERT STERLING

Slowly

Things change, __ plans fail, __ you look for love __ on a grand-
Time flies, __ hearts turn __ a lit-tle bit wis-er from les-

- er scale. __ Storms rise, __ hopes fade, __ and
- sons learned. __ But some-times __ weak-ness __ wins, __ and

you place your bets __ on an-oth-er day. __ }
you lose your foot-hold __ once __ a-gain. __ }

When the go-in' gets tough, __ when the ride's

LOVE ONE ANOTHER

Words and Music by WAYNE KIRKPATRICK
and MICHAEL W. SMITH

I had a dream that I was speak-
It was a sim-ple con-clu-

-ing with a proph-et from the land of wise
-sion, but I thought that it was rath-er pro-found,

in a crowd of peo-ple from the land of trou-bled hearts.
just a fun-da-men-tal law that we should all live by.

MERCY CAME RUNNING

Words and Music by DAVE CLARK,
DON KOCH and DAN DEAN

Once there was a ho-ly__ place,__
Once there was a bro-ken__ heart,__

ev - i - dence__ of God's em - brace;__
way too hu - man from the__ start;__

SAY THE NAME

Words and Music by MARGARET BECKER
and CHARLIE PEACOCK

95

SIGNS OF LIFE

Words and Music by
STEVEN CURTIS CHAPMAN

WE TRUST IN THE NAME OF THE LORD OUR GOD

Words and Music by
STEVEN CURTIS CHAPMAN

WHERE YOU BELONG/
TURN YOUR EYES UPON JESUS

WHERE YOU BELONG

Words and Music by PETER FURLER
and STEVE TAYLOR

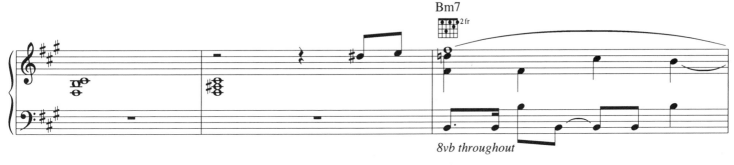

When you're dull __ from all __ that glit-
used to __ the cold __ for so

TURN YOUR EYES UPON JESUS
Words and Music by HELEN H. LEMMEL

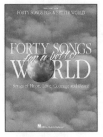
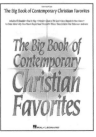

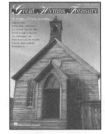

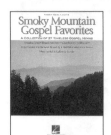